SURVIVAL WRITING:
Staying Alive on Paper

Stephen D. Gladis
Education/Communication Arts Unit
FBI Academy
Quantico, Virginia

All author's proceeds go to Heroes Inc., which
financially supports the education of slain law
enforcement officers' children.

KENDALL/HUNT PUBLISHING COMPANY
2460 Kerper Boulevard P.O. Box 539 Dubuque, Iowa 52004-0539

Printed in the United States of America
10 9 8 7 6 5

To my wife Donna and daughters Kimberly and Jessica.

Contents

Acknowledgments

My sincerest thanks to Dr. Donald Gallehr, Co-director of the National Writing Project and Director of the Northern Virginia Writing Project, for his positive and continued support. To Karen Hickman, Don's "right arm" at the Project, for her help and understanding. To Pat Solley, editor at the FBI Academy, for her keen eye and kind words. To Colleen Baldwin for her infinite patience and skill with the word processor. To Donna, my best friend and darling wife, for putting up with a clacking typewriter every morning at 4:00 A.M., a tired and sometimes moody husband, and a string of lost weekends sacrificed to revision.

Foreword

Several years ago a graduate student of mine asked if I thought she could handle an editing job for a local organization. I knew she had had courses in writing and editing and had years of experience working with adults. I told her to take the job—she could handle it.

Within a month she returned with a manual she had been assigned to revise. On the first page she had changed the phrase "moisture delivery mechanism" to "rain." Her supervisor, however, insisted that she keep the original wording. Why? "Because it's better."

Unfortunately, such stories are more the rule than the exception. Most people on the job today received their instruction in writing at a period in American education when we knew relatively little about teaching writing. The first major research, Janet Emig's *The Composing Process of Twelfth Graders* (1971) launched a series of studies on the writing processes of children and adults which revolutionized the way writing is taught in the schools.

This revolution is now seeping into the business world, into the writing of adults on the job. This book, reflecting current research, is among the very first to address the employee who wishes to improve his writing. It is written in a fast-paced, enjoyable style spiked with specific examples only an insider could develop.

Steve Gladis knows from extensive experience that a writer's first draft contains the roadsigns for revision. His book interprets these signs and provides a map with the best roads highlighted. He describes a writing process which is productive and humane. And he addresses the corporate bottom line—the enormous waste in time and money produced by poor writing. Consequently, he includes a section on dictation and encourages writers to collaborate.

I recommend that the reader scan the whole book before "studying" any one section. Mr. Gladis' new world of the proficient business writer holds together best when all parts support the whole. Once you've made this book your own, give a copy to your supervisor. We don't need another "moisture delivery mechanism."

Donald R. Gallehr,
Co-Director of the
National Writing Project
and Director of the
Northern Virginia
Writing Project

Preface

REVISION: RETURN ON YOUR ORIGINAL INVESTMENT

What if Thomas Edison had refused to revise his original plan for the light bulb? What if Henry Ford had balked at changing his first design for mass production of the automobile? If they had not made significant revisions of their original products, most of us would still be reading by candlelight and walking to work. "Revision" is one of the toughest words in our language to accept because it implies giving up, at least in part, an original idea, design, or structure—and few of us are willing to give up familiar things without a fight.

Just as Edison and Ford were successful because they revised their plans, to be successful, writers also must continually revise. Writers begin with a torrent of information, direct it into a flood of words, and trim back the words to a stream of well-crafted language. Writing requires both a giving and a taking away, an ebb and flow. The result is language that is clear, direct, and meaningful.

Because business writing informs, explains, or persuades, it must have clarity and direction. Business readers are customers who must make decisions and spend money based on written language. Writing that is vague, indirect, or meaningless to the customer is useless and unprofitable. Writing is part of the competitive process in business. It's not just a socially acceptable skill—it's a survival skill. Whether it's a resumé, a marketing proposal, or an annual stockholders' report, good business writing can drive you to the heights of success or the depths of failure.

Today, unfortunately, we face tremendous time pressures in the business world. As managers, we must write quickly under extreme deadline pressures and have little time to rewrite. After a while, not rewriting becomes such a habit that even when we have time, we often don't make the effort. Eventually, many of us forget some basic grammatical and revising skills learned years ago.

This book attempts to help you solve that problem. First, it's geared to the businessperson who's in a hurry. Second, it highlights problem areas. I've surveyed the most common errors made in business communications and have demonstrated ways to correct them. The rules are briefly and simply stated; the examples are concrete and relate to business; and the analysis is direct and simple.

WHO SHOULD USE THIS BOOK

Businesspeople Who Must Write Well

If writing is important to your career development, this book can help. It focuses on how to strengthen writing and addresses many of the most common problems facing you daily. This book will help you hone a skill that may be rusty.

Anyone Learning to Write in the Business World

This book is also geared to newcomers in the business world. With concrete, business-related examples, the book offers direct application for even the newest employees.

Anyone Who Likes to Write

This book is a tune-up manual for those already able to write. Covering structure, grammar, syntax, and style, it will reinforce old skills and offer new writing strategies for your consideration.

HOW TO USE THIS BOOK

Use It as a Grammatical Review Book

Designated chapters treat those grammatical problems most common to business. They are written in small chunks that will fit comfortably in the nooks and crannies of a busy day. Each rule is accompanied by simple, usable examples.

Use It as a Desktop Reference

The book is compact, simple to use, and short. It can fit in your back pocket and easily slip into an attaché case. It has mainframe capability at portable PC size.

Use It as a Revision Manual

The book will strengthen your writing and revising. Because it is brief, you can read the book before you put pen to paper and skim it again after you've finished the first draft—a practice which will add quality to good writing and polish excellent writing even more.

Use It as an Instructional Aid

Give copies to new employees. This practice will help set a writing standard for your company and give each new employee a uniform style and reference manual.

Business is an evolutionary process in which only the best survive. You know that products are improved and refined because consumers demand quality. But do you know that business writing is evaluated by the same standard? Although business deadlines and schedules might not leave you much time to reread and revise unclear writing, you must clarify it or lose your customers. Make sure your first chance to communicate with the reader is a clear, well-constructed, revised edition; otherwise, you may have no second chance.

Use Direct, Useful Verbs

1

Real men may not eat quiche and real women may not pump gas, but real men and women do use action words. In any sentence, verbs carry the action. They give the sentence life and motion and set the pulse for written language.

MAKE VERBS WORK

Verbs provide a strong source of energy for business writing, particularly in their simplest forms: base verbs. Base verbs such as "hit," "throw," "drink," and "stand," all convey the purest and most direct meaning of the verb. When the base verb is converted to another part of speech, however, the strength fades and the color pales by comparison.

Weakened Form: *Hitting* the ball over the fence, John scored the winning run.

Base Verb: John *hit* the ball over the fence and scored the winning run.

The first example just doesn't convey a strong visual message because the verb is converted from an action word to a modifier (of John). Camouflaging the base verb reduces the action of the sentence. In the second example you can hear the crack of the bat and see the ball fly over the infield and beyond the reach of the outfielders as it clears the fence.

BE STRONG, KEEP ORDER

A good simple sentence is the cornerstone of solid business writing because it gives strength, clarity, and direction to language. Normal word order in a sentence is subject-verb-object: the verb cements the relationship between the subject and object, and grounds the three on a strong foundation. When that order changes, however, the relationships are less clear because the construction is weaker. In a sense, the foundation has cracked. Consider the following:

Out of Order: *Authorization* to pay the bill was given by the manager. (10 words)

Natural: The manager *authorized* the bill payment. (6 words)

The first sentence lacks direction and force because the order is inverted and camouflaged as a noun.

DON'T HIDE VERBS

Camouflaged verbs are weak because they're abstract—you can't see, touch, taste, smell, or feel them. Consider two people who have just agreed to a contract after long and tedious hours of negotiation. Read the following two sentences and decide which one works better to convey meaning most directly:

Muffled Negotiations: After long hours of negotiations, labor leaders and management officials came to an agreement and the contract was signed.

When Two Agree: After long hours of negotiations, labor leaders and management officials shook hands and agreed to sign the contract.

The first sentence is difficult to envision. Most abstracts such as "agreement" are tough to visualize because they float somewhere beyond our senses. A handshake is a different matter, however. We shake hands every day to represent agreement. A handshake is concrete and familiar—an international sign that people agree.

Base verbs save money for the company because they are concise, direct, and easy to comprehend. Any time you can save paperwork and increase understanding, you're putting money in the bank. Look at these examples:

A Cost Overrun: An *illustration* of the profit and loss statement was made by the accountant by the *utilization* of charts. (18 words)

An Economical Version: The accountant *used* charts to *illustrate* the profit and loss statement. (11 words)

2

Besides being brief, the second example is easier to understand and more to the point; as a result, the reader invests less and gets more in return—a perfect business deal.

To help you clear up clouded, weak writing, try this simple but effective exercise. Read a page of manuscript, underlining every word that ends with -ent, -ant, -ion, -ment, -ence, -ance, -ency. Review the passage by deciding if the underlined words can be changed to the base form of the verb to improve the text. In most cases you'll find that the meaning will become more direct and forceful. Try the underlining exercise on the following paragraph:

> **Bloated Language:** The company came to an agreement with labor to offer employment to minority groups across the board. The decision to offer jobs was reached on Sunday afternoon and the implementation was scheduled for the following Monday. The minority groups made a statement that, pending implementation of the new policy, they would withhold official comment. (55 words)

You should have underlined the following words: agreement, employment, implementation, statement, and implementation.

> **Trimmed Language:** On Sunday the company agreed to employ all minority groups. The minority groups, however, would not comment on the program before it began on Monday. (25 words)

The first paragraph contains 55 words and the second only 25 words—that's saving more than fifty percent. The first paragraph sounds fuzzy and vague, while the second is clear and forceful.

The following is a short list of commonly camouflaged words and their base verbs:

Camouflaged Words	Base Verbs
settlement	settle
assistance	assist
consideration	consider
arbitration	arbitrate
resistant	resist
negligent	neglect
performance	perform

When you're trying to project the image of a company that deals straight and gets the job done without any frills or fanfare, which style do you think serves the company best?

KEEP YOUR VOICE ACTIVE

If real businesspeople should use base verbs, they surely should use the active voice as well. Why go halfway? To be direct and vigorous, use the active voice. Remember this cliché: Actives speak louder than passives. In the active voice, the subject does the action. In the passive voice, the subject is acted upon.

Passive: The chef was fired by John. (6 words)

Active: John fired the chef. (4 words)

In the second sentence John acts, but in the first the chef is acted upon. Not only is the second more direct and consistent with the intended meaning, but it's also shorter. Brevity is like a nontaxable fringe benefit of the active voice.

The passive voice, however, provides good camouflage and a safe haven for company bureaucrats seeking ambiguity, anonymity, and obscurity. The writer who uses the passive voice avoids authorship and responsibility. Unfortunately, the passive voice has become a tradition in bureaucracies that has been passed down to each new generation like a curse. The tradition has become so entrenched that use of the active voice often is looked upon as odd. Oops! I slipped into the passive, so you might note that the passive can be legitimate, especially if it varies the language. It's okay to use it for variety, but be careful that it doesn't become the norm.

Indefinite Approach: The regulations were approved this past week and will be implemented immediately.

Definite Style: I approved the regulations last week and will implement them immediately.

Reading the first sentence, the Chairman of the Board will not know who to call about the impact of the decision. The second sentence is not only more definite, but also more personal with the use of "I." Save time and fix responsibility. Make it personal. Be direct and clear, and use the active voice—unless you're trying to cover some obviously poor move. Then by all means use the passive voice, call in sick, or go on vacation.

WATCH OUT FOR *BY'S*

Passive language has crept so insidiously into our writing that it is often difficult to identify. To help you spot the obvious or hidden passives, use this aid: watch for all the *by's* in your sentence—even the implied *by's*.

Passive: The redistricting of the sales territories was approved (*by someone*) and sent (*by someone*) to the president for approval. The plan was reviewed *by* the president's special assistant and finally approved *by* the president.

Active: The sales board approved the redistricting of the sales territories and sent it to the president. His special assistant reviewed the plan before the president approved it.

The second paragraph tells the reader who approved what and gets through the matter quickly and with no confusion.

The active voice is the standard rallying cry of any dynamic leader. If you use the active voice, your writing will clearly, directly, and forcefully represent you and your company. Don't "soft pedal" your wares. Ride to success by being more direct. Use the active voice.

BEWARE OF LINKS THAT LEECH

While most verbs convey action or state of being, some verbs merely link the subject to its modifier or state of being. These verbs, called linking verbs, are dangerous because they lack the vitality of active verbs. Read the following examples and see:

Drained: John *was happy.*

Lively: John *laughed* so hard that tears came to his eyes.

In the first example, *was happy* expresses joy, but only in a broad, bland way; it is unspecific and weak. On the other hand, *laughed* in the second example depicts something you can see and hear; it's more specific because it indicates the intensity of expression. Beware of linking verbs that steal the zest from your writing and sap its strength. Here is a list of links that leech:

A List of Links that Leech:

To be (is, are, was, etc.)	Feel	Taste
Appear	Grow	Smell
Become	Act	Sound
Seem	Look	

In the business of writing, verbs are worth their weight in gold. Strong verbs give meaning and direction to the sentence and so add value to your message. Cut liabilities, shore up values, and increase your profits: use base verbs, avoid the passive voice, and, where possible, shun linking verbs.

Keep Sentences Short   2

When is preparing food like writing? Some would say, "When you eat your words." Actually, writing is a process like food preparation—and both take time and cost money. Consider the following scenario: your boss has just told you to answer a letter that he received from the ABC Company complaining about a defective widget sold by your company and seeking a refund. Look now at how the process of writing a response costs your company money.

First, you spend 10–15 minutes to decipher the boss' note on the bottom of the page. Finally, you relent and go to the source: the boss. After a longwinded sermon on what it means to be a self starter, the boss translates his comment: "Handle this." Bewildered, you return to your office.

Pen in hand, you begin. You stop, reread the letter, and wonder if the boss really has any idea of either the problem or what he wants done. After a trip to the company library for background information, you lunch with a buddy and relate your stimulating conversation with the boss. Your friend offers to give you a copy of a similar letter he wrote a week ago. Though the topic differs, the format helps you get started and you write an initial draft. After revisions, helpful editing from your buddy, and a few tips from your secretary, you finish the letter and pass it along to the boss. He sends it back to you with a few additions and deletions of his own. Eventually, you send the letter.

THE ECONOMIC IMPACT OF WRITING

If you determined the total processing costs of your letter, you'd be surprised. Some current estimates range conservatively between $15 and $20 per page for typical business communications. When you write, therefore, you want the process to be short and efficient, and the final product, succinct, accurate, and understandable. If not, your company pays dearly.

If you multiply the millions of letters and memoranda written every day in government and business by an average of $17, you can see the fortune to be saved by trimming back the flow of unnecessary words. Suddenly, the writing process is a moneysaving event.

THE RULE OF TWENTY

Tackling the paperwork of business is intimidating to the average person even when all biorhythms are right. The secret is to start small: begin with the basic sentence. To contain the verbal explosion in business, employ the Rule of Twenty words for your sentences. Readers can't easily comprehend long and tedious sentences. They rapidly lose interest. Keep sentence length to twenty words—or two typed lines—and you'll keep the reader. The Rule of Twenty necessarily trims back the fat and exposes your message. Consider the following example:

Word Proliferation: This letter is written relative to our personal computer that was the subject of your most recent inquiry concerning our manufacturer's rebate which we do give to such well-regarded customers like your company which has enjoyed a long-standing relationship with our firm. (44 words)

This sentence would challenge even the most interested reader. Long, overwritten, and boring, it loses its thrust because of its wordiness. To help you cast off its excess baggage, use the Rule of Twenty. Begin by underlining all the key words—those words essential to your message. In this sentence you probably will have underlined computer, manufacturer's rebate, well-regarded customers, and our firm. Next, write the sentence in more direct language, still keeping the message that good companies get rebates.

Economical Version: Yes, our firm will offer you a rebate because you're one of our preferred customers. (15 words)

The new shortened sentence is only fifteen words long. We've saved twenty-nine words. That's a cost reduction in anyone's book. The Rule of Twenty, however, is not chiseled in granite and should be used only as a guideline and not as a commandment. Remember, when trimming back excess: underline key words, choose language that is active and expressive, and keep your sentences to approximately twenty words.

THE WAY TO BE BRIEF

To help you trim back excess words, you should:

Cut Prepositional Phrases

These causes of grammatical obesity are as fattening as chocolate-covered cherries. For example:

Obese	Trim
Along the lines of	Like
As of this date	Today
At the present time	Now
For the purpose of	Because
Inasmuch as	For, as
In order to	To
In relation to	About, concerning
In the event that	If
On the basis of	By
On a few occasions	Occasionally
Subsequent to	After
With reference to	About
With regard to	About, concerning
With respect to	On, about

To cut back wordy prepositional phrases, underline all prepositions such as: by, with, at, in, to, on, for, between, and from. Then sharpen your editorial carver and slice the fat away from the lean.

Delete Double-Dealing Words

Wasted time costs money in any business. Duplication of effort, whether on the job or in writing, wastes time for everyone concerned. *Tautologies* are word clusters with overlapping meanings. They duplicate efforts, bloat language, and waste time. No reader needs to be impaled twice to get the point. The following are examples of tautologies and efficient solutions to them:

Duplicative	Efficient
Advance Planning	Planning
Ask the question	Ask
Continue on	Continue
Cooperate with	Cooperate

Duplicative	*Efficient*
Each separate incident	Each incident
Protest against	Protest
Definite decision	Decision
Free gift	Gift
Free pass	Pass
Invited Guests	Guests
Old Adage	Adage
Personal friend	Friend
Dash quickly	Dash
True Facts	Facts
Reason Why	Reason

To ferret out tautologies, look at the following example for non-essential words, and you'll find at least part of the tautology:

Tautology Trial: During the anti-trust trial the president gave the true facts about the conglomerate's merger plans.

Note that *facts* is a word essential to the sentence but *true* isn't. You're likely to find tautologies lurking among the unnecessary words and often right next to an essential word. With a sharp eye you can spot these duplicators, then flush them out of the sentence.

Beware of the Passive Voice

As we discussed in the previous chapter, use of the passive voice not only will sap your writing of its vitality but also will bloat your writing. The passive voice construction adds extra words—verbs of being as well as qualifiers—and it often leaves the reader with questions of authorship.

Original Bid: It is recommended that the company accept the bid submitted by the contractor. (13 words)

"Who recommends?" is the first problem that the sentence poses for the reader. The second problem is that the writer must explain which bid to accept, and must use extra language to do so.

Final Bid: I recommend we accept the contractor's bid. (7 words)

This sentence has neither questions nor explanations because they're unnecessary; more, the sentence is almost fifty percent shorter. Increased clarity and word economy are money in the bank for any company.

The recent inflation in our economy is reflected in our writing. Just as prices increase, eroding our buying power, so do words multiply, eroding the sense and power of our written communications. When you see word clusters creeping into your text, stop the flow and cut the upward spiral by leaving them out.

Avoid Abstractions and Use Concrete Language

3

THE SIN OF OVERWRITING

Most of us remember the Bible story of how God gave Moses the Ten Commandments on a mountaintop. God etched the Commandments on two large stone tablets, and they became the best known laws in history. Why? Because they're direct, concrete, to the point, and they make sense. Just consider one of the Commandments as an example: *Thou shalt not kill.* Though the language is dated, it leaves no doubt in the reader's mind about what's expected.

On the other hand, what if the Commandment read like this:

> Having been a party of or accomplice to the willful taking of human life, whether patricide, fratricide or homicide of any type, and whether the deed be premeditated or spontaneous, such act presents the gravest of moral, ethical, and spiritual ramifications for the malefactor.

First, Moses would have needed a moving van to haul the tablets from the mountaintop. Second, no one would have ever understood the Ten Commandments.

Abstractions usually confuse readers. This is not to say that abstractions have no place in our written language. To the contrary, abstractions represent man's ability to deal with pure ideas and to universalize. But, except for the philosopher, words lose clarity as they lose their color and sense.

The "tangible" words come to us through the senses—we hear them, see them, reach out and touch them. As we move away from the sensual experiences and toward intellectual ones, however, we create abstractions. Since each of us forms abstractions differently, diversity and confusion often result. By moving out from the senses, writing often loses its focus, leaving the reader behind in the process.

THE "RIPPLE EFFECT" OF ABSTRACTIONS

Abstractions are like the concentric ripples that form when you throw a rock into a clear pond. A rock entering the water is like the solid, concrete image. Once the rock breaks the surface, shock waves are sent out in concentric ripples, each bigger than its predecessor yet less defined. To illustrate the "ripple effect" in language, let's consider something critical to business: money.

To begin with the most concrete image of money—analogous to the rock splashing into the water—picture a new one dollar bill. You can see it and feel it. You can fold it, put it in your wallet, and buy two candy bars with it. It's real. But as the ripples move out from the 6" × 2½", green, one dollar bill, the images get soft, unfocused, and more difficult to comprehend. Look at the following list to see the ripple effect on money:

1. dollar bill
2. folding cash
3. money
4. funds
5. currency
6. medium of exchange

You can see that as language moves away from the concrete dollar bill, it devalues rapidly and its meaning is obscured in the process.

Avoid unnecessary abstractions in your writing by employing the "Keep It Simple" rule. When in doubt about using abstractions, journalists ask these basic questions: Who, What, Why, Where, When, and How? Answer these questions about each piece you write and your writing will bristle with concrete language. Look at the following sentences:

Devalued Language: The business executive traveled out of town to attend a meeting last week.

In this example, abstractions and generalities are overused. *Executive, traveled, out of town, meeting,* and *last week* are all abstract words that tell only a vague story. Because of abstractions, the reader naturally asks: Who went out of town? How did that person travel? Where and why did that person leave? The questions raised by abstractions bog down the reader and waste too much time on images that should be in clear focus from the start.

Value-Based Language: John Sloane flew to Denver last Thursday to attend the annual stockholders' meeting.

In the second example, the questions raised by the first are answered merely by using direct, concrete language. Each critical word is like a rock splashing into the water breaking the surface. This sentence has no ripple effect: it tells the readers everything they want to know.

EXCESSIVE VARIATION

Another cause of fuzziness in business writing is excessive variation. To understand this, you must think back to elementary school days when a teacher warned you not to use the same word twice in the same sentence. That instruction was primarily focused on improving students' vocabularies. But in an adult world, constant variations can and often do lead to confusion. Consider the following sentences:

Variation on a Theme: One *executive* in the company received a handsome bonus, while another *supervisor* got a lesser amount, and yet another *manager* got even less than the others. (26 words)

Cleared Up: The three company managers received different bonuses. (7 words)

In the first example, *executive, manager,* and *supervisor* are intended to mean the same thing—but the reader is not really sure. The first sentence avoids repeating the same word three times, but confuses the reader in the process. The reader will naturally wonder: Are these three company officials of the same executive level? The reader is forced to weigh each variation against the others and in many cases is driven to an unabridged dictionary for definitions of esoteric words. Airing your knowledge of unfamiliar words at the expense of the reader is a mistake.

THE VALUE OF CONCRETE LANGUAGE

People read to learn, not to be impressed, insulted, or belittled. Pedantic overwriting, a close cousin of excessive variation, can also inhibit meaning. Of course, I'm not suggesting that you write only in monosyllables. Some language variation is useful, in fact, because it adds spice to writing and makes the text more palatable. Just remember that too spicy a dish is indigestible. Read the following examples:

Stuffy Stuff: Due largely to a paucity of concern, this day has been summarily terminated.

Aired Out: Because of a lack of interest, today has been canceled.

These two versions need no explanation. We've all been guilty of showing off. Avoid confusion for the reader by using clear, familiar language to convey a specific message.

Good business operates in a concrete world. To be effective in business you must communicate your company's ideas in words that people understand quickly and clearly. The surest and simplest way to relate to others is through the senses—words that help you touch, taste, smell, see, and hear. Use concrete and familiar language; strive to communicate, not necessarily to dominate.

Keep Related Words Together 4

There is a natural order to things in the business world: expenses usually come before profits, design before production, and marketing before sales. Language also has an order. Standard word order in the English language is Subject-Verb-Object.

(subject) (verb)   (object)
The banker   gave the money to him.

English, in fact, relies on word order for meaning. Consider the following sentences if you have any doubt:

BOW: The dog bit the man.

WOW: The man bit the dog.

IMPORTANT WORDS GO FIRST OR LAST

Saving the best until last works as well in language as in life—particularly if you want to emphasize a word. If you want to emphasize a particular word in a sentence, put it at the very end. Or, you can place it at the very beginning. If you choose a place other than these two locations, your emphasis will be flattened somewhere in the middle.

Suppose you wanted to emphasize to your boss that certain efforts have resulted in big profits for the company. The key word is *profits*. Consider the impact of the next two sentences:

Muffled Profits: In the recent past our efforts to increase *profits* by cutting overhead expenses have been successful.

Roaring Profits: Recently, the reduced overhead expenses have increased *profits*.

In the first example, *profit* is imbedded in the sentence, and the reader must either reread it to get your point or lose it among the words.

The second sentence, however, makes sure that the reader gets the point by placing *profit* in an obvious and prominent position. Just remember the old axiom: Position is everything in life!

MISPLACED MODIFIERS

One of the most common errors in business writing is to misplace modifiers. Adjectives, adverbs, phrases, and clauses all modify or describe something in a sentence. When misplaced, they modify the wrong thing and mislead the reader:

Misplaced Modifier: *Typing the report furiously,* the boss interrupted *me.*

Realigned: *While typing the report, I* was interrupted by the boss.

The first sentence overworks the boss, who probably couldn't type even if his or her life depended on it. By moving the typing closer to the typist, *you* get the job done faster.

As a rule, keep the modifiers and related words together in a sentence to avoid confusion like this:

Poor Management: The CEO discussed filling the vacancies in the mail room with the senior partners.

In this sentence, it looks as if the boss is going to place some pretty high-priced talent in entry-level positions. What the writer probably intended to say was:

Unruffled Partners: The CEO and the senior partners discussed the vacancies in the mail room.

By moving the senior partners closer to the boss, you'll save yourself an explanation memo to some ruffled executives.

Words

The simple way to solve ambiguity that arises from misplaced words is to underline the modifiers in question. Underlining helps you see the distance between the modifier and the word being modified. Any gaps between the two will show up immediately.

Misplaced Salesman: The <u>salesman</u> made an important sale to a major client <u>using visual aids</u>.

In this sentence, the client seems to be using the visual aids instead of the salesman, which is pretty good salesmanship if you can do it! The following sentence, however, is probably more accurate:

Good Salesmanship: <u>Using visual aids</u>, the <u>salesman</u> made an important sale to a major client.

Squinters

When modifiers can modify words on either side of themselves, they are said to "squint," since they don't focus well on the word they should modify. When in doubt, place the modifier near the word you want to modify—and as far as possible from any other word with which it could be mistakenly linked:

Squinting: The committee which was studying redistricting of sales territories *yesterday* made its recommendations to the national sales manager.

Open Eyed: The committee studying redistricting of sales territories made its recommendations to the national sales manager *yesterday.*

After reading the first example, you might think that such a major reorganization was done rather haphazardly and in a rush because *yesterday* seems to modify *studying* as well as *made.* Yesterday, however, refers to when the final report was made and not to the duration or time spent studying. That's a big difference! If you were the boss, wouldn't you have some questions about the quality of the report after reading the first sentence?

Phrases and Clauses

Dangling phrases or clauses hang freely without being clearly connected to whatever they are intended to modify. They're misplaced modifiers that can lead to unwanted humor and confusion among readers:

Nervous Boss: After straightening his tie, combing his hair, and clearing his throat, the *boss* was briefed by the newest partner in the firm.

New Partner: After straightening his tie, combing his hair, and clearing his throat, the newest partner briefed the boss.

In the first sentence, the boss seemed to be going to a lot of trouble to impress the new man. The second sentence makes more sense. When a phrase or clause comes at the beginning of a sentence, the word modified should come after the comma or as close to it as possible to avoid gaps and confusion.

Sentences

A gap in a White House tape caused a certain president some real problems. A gap in your taxable income causes problems, and a gap between your pants and shirt causes embarrassment. Remember one simple rule to avoid confusion in writing: gaps cause trouble. Keep subjects with verbs and objects with verbs to avoid gaps and confusion.

Generally, gaps between subject and verb, verb and object, or parts of verb phrases confuse the reader.

> **The Gap:** The free *trip* to Hawaii, which was the grand prize given each year by the TDY Company for the salesman who sold the most widgets, *was given* to Sam Jones.

The reader gets lost enroute while trying to get the trip to Hawaii and Sam Jones together because the subject, *trip,* and the verb, *was given,* are separated by a wide gap. Try this sentence as a solution:

> **Closing the Gap:** The *trip* to Hawaii *was given* to Sam Jones for selling the most widgets for the TDY Company this year.

This sentence helps bridge the gap to Hawaii by getting the subject and verb together. Sam gets his deserved reward more quickly—and clearly.

Consider the following sentence and try to find the gap between the main verb and its verb phrase:

> **Gap:** The managing editor tried, for literally years and years while employed at the newspaper in the editorial group, to be objective and fair.

By splitting the verb *tried to be,* the writer creates a gap in this sentence which may lead the reader to think the entire editorial group is trying to be objective and fair. The reader simply has to vault over too much territory to land safely on the other side. Shorten the verbal gap like this:

> **Bridged:** While employed in the newspaper's editorial group, the *managing editor tried to be* objective and fair.

Now there is little question who's trying to be objective and fair.

Sort out the verb and its object if you can:

Hedging: The Chairman of the Board announced, after discussing the wonderful hotel accommodations, the fabulous social galas for the week, and the golf and tennis arrangements, a deficit for the year.

This sentence makes it appear like the golf and tennis arrangements had a deficit and not our unfortunate company. Try this revision:

Facing the Music: After discussing the wonderful hotel accommodations, the fabulous social galas for the week, and the golf and tennis arrangements, the Chairman of the Board *announced a deficit* for the year.

If you are trying to hide the deficit from the stockholders, by all means use the first sentence! If, however, you want to make sense and not confuse your reader, use the second sentence.

To avoid confusion and to increase clarity:

- Keep related words together.
- Stress words by placing them at the beginning or end of the sentence.
- Keep modifiers close to the words they modify.
- Underline to find your word gaps.
- Don't let modifiers dangle.
- Keep subjects and verbs as well as verbs and objects together.

Don't Shift Number, Tense, Sex, Subject, or Point of View

5

Shifting galloping horses midstream may be all right for cowboys, but don't try it when writing or you may get all wet. Anytime you shift subject, number, verb, tense, or point of view in a sentence, you stand a good chance of dumping your readers as well.

SHIFTING NUMBERS

Pronouns refer back to nouns. He, she, it, we, they, and other pronouns substitute for nouns and lend variety to your writing by avoiding the needless repetition of nouns. When used incorrectly, however, a pronoun can stop the readers in their tracks.

Dwindling Investors: The *investors* were interested in buying the property until *he* saw the city dump adjacent to it.

Consistent Investors: The *investors* were interested in buying the property until *they* saw the city dump adjacent to it.

In the first example, the *investors* shifted to *he,* and suddenly a conglomerate became an individual. The reader gets confused and certainly loses confidence in a group of investors that dwindles so quickly to a single *he.*

The second example starts with a group, *investors,* and ends with a group, *they.* If you had to throw your lot in with either of these two sentences, which would you choose? Make sure that pronouns both agree with the words they precede and relate to them (antecedents). Leave the shifting to your sports car, not your writing.

INDEFINITE PRONOUNS AND INDEFINITE LANGUAGE

An indefinite pronoun does *not* refer to a specific person or thing. Pronouns such as each, either, everyone, everybody, somebody, and nobody are only some examples of indefinite pronouns. All are singular.

Since they are often mistaken for the plural, they are often the source of errors in writing. Consider the following examples:

Definitely Confusing: *Everyone* brought *their* coats to the meeting.

Clear Cut: *Everyone* brought *his* or *her* coat to the meeting.

The first example creates a confusing image for the reader. No one is sure whether each person has several coats or the group owns a few coats. The second sentence makes it clear that each person brought one coat. Indefinite pronouns don't have to cause indefinite language if you stay on track and use the singular.

COLLECTIVE NOUNS

You remember the Class of '42 and the Olympic Team? How about the Senate and the House of Representatives? The committee, the group, the council or the class? They're all collective nouns. When you use them in a singular way, use a singular pronoun; use a plural pronoun if you're referring to each individual in the group. And, oh yes, be consistent:

All For One: The *committee* on waste *works* well, and it saves the company inestimable amounts of money.

One For All: The *committee vote their* consciences on all issues and *are* very independent.

In the first example, the *committee* is used collectively and, therefore, takes the singular pronoun *it* as well as the singular verbs *saves* and *works*. The second example uses the *committee* to refer to the individual members of the committee; hence, committee is used in a plural sense and requires the plural pronoun *their* and the plural verbs *vote* and *are*.

SHIFTING TENSES

Time means money in business. Deadlines rule industry—and if you miss them constantly you might well consider the virtues of unemployment. For executives, time is especially precious; a host of books and hundreds of courses teach the businessperson how to save it.

And when you shift tenses, you force the reader to reread, to reflect, to refigure in order to understand your message. If the reader refuses to waste such time, your message is lost forever. Time is limited—don't waste yours or the reader's. Pick a tense and stick to it.

Timing Problem: The Chief Executive Officer *studied* the proposal thoroughly and *makes* a wise decision.

In Gear: The Chief Executive Officer *studied* the proposal thoroughly and *made* a wise decision.

The first example shifts tenses from the past tense, *studied,* to the present tense, *makes,* leaving the reader caught in a time warp and uncertain *when* the action takes place. The second keeps the action in the past tense, *studied* and *made.*

CHANGING VOICES

Another annoying shift in writing that confuses most readers is the shift from the active voice to the passive voice. To most readers it's as immature as a teenage prank and as laughable as the squeak of an adolescent's voice.

Voice Change: The committee chairperson *opened* the meeting after the notes *had been reviewed.*

Straight Talk: The committee chairperson *opened* the meeting after *she* reviewed the notes.

The first sentence causes the reader to wonder who reviewed the notes. The second example leaves no doubt: the sentence is clearer; the reader stays with you and certainly gains confidence in the chairperson. Speak loud and clear and speak with one voice.

Words like businessman, chairman, workman, and others creep into our writing and reflect the male bias in our society and, in particular, the business world. These sex-biased words presume that only men populate the workplace and, worse yet, that only men occupy positions of importance and power. Sexist language denies women their status both in the workplace and in your writing, and it should be scrupulously avoided. Here are some tips that will help:

Avoid Sex-Dominated Idioms
—a man-sized job
—a real he-man
—a weak sister
—the manly thing to do
—a woman's touch

Use Plural Subjects to Avoid Sex-Biased Pronouns

Not: Each *editor* took his reporters to meet the publisher for the first time.

But: All the *editors* took *their* reporters to meet the publisher for the first time.

Avoid Male-Dominated Titles

Not	*But*
Policeman	Police Officer
Committeeman	Member of the committee
Workman	Worker

Use Job Titles to Avoid Servile Sex Roles

Not: The *woman* behind the counter offered *her* help by giving directions to the customer.

But: The *attendant* helped by giving directions to the customer.

Omit the Pronoun Where Possible

Not: If treated well by management, the American worker does *his* best on the job.

But: If treated well by management, the American worker does very well on the job.

Use *He and She* or *He/She*

Use this technique only as a last resort because it is awkward and contrived. It is, however, better than a sexist alternative.

Not: Each worker turned in *his* hours to the timekeeper.

But: Each worker turned in *his or her* hours to the timekeeper.

CHANGING THE SUBJECT

Changing the subject or topic in business is sometimes a useful tactic. It will definitely throw people off course, divert attention, and shift the emphasis to less dangerous areas—that is often the safest course. If, however, you want to be readily understood by others, stick to the subject in all of your sentences:

Subject Shift: *Mr. Edwards* corrected the confusing report and the *report* was retyped.

Consistent: *Mr. Edwards* corrected the confusing report and then *he* had it retyped.

In the first example, the subject shifts from *Mr. Edwards* to *report*. The reader wonders if Mr. Edwards or someone else typed the report. You should also note that a confusing shift in subject often accompanies the passive voice, as is true in this example. The second sentence smooths out the bumps and keeps the subject consistent throughout the sentence. *Mr. Edwards* and *he*.

A MATTER OF POINT OF VIEW

You may remember that point of view is the perspective from which a story is told. For example, if the narrator is one of the main actors in a story, he uses the first person, *I* or *we*, as the point of view. If the narrator is directly addressing the reader, he uses the second person and says *you*. Finally, if the narrator is telling a story about someone else performing the action, he writes about *he, she, it,* or *they*. Writers will often shift the point of view in midsentence and leave the reader wondering who is doing what to whom:

Point Shift: The *boss* said that when *I* read the report of the auditors, *you* could see the obvious errors that *we* had been making.

Right on Point: The *boss* said that when *he* read the auditor's report *he* could see the obvious errors that the company had made.

The first example shifts from the *boss* to *I* to *you* and back to *we*—and the reader falls between the cracks, unable to decide who's in charge of this sentence. In the second example, it's clear that the *boss* is in charge. The point of view clearly is his own.

Shifts in point of view are common, particularly in longer pieces of writing. These shifts usually occur when the writer loses sight of who is telling the story and what effect he wishes to make. Keep your writing on track through faithful proofreading and by asking yourself who's telling the story.

There are a lot of shifts in life. There are shifts in the tide and shifts in the land. We work different shifts and often shift positions to get comfortable during a boring meeting. We know shifty businesspeople and try to avoid them. We experience violent shifts in the stock market and try to escape with our skin.

There are shifts in football, cars, trains, planes, and buses. We shift, they shift, and you probably shift, too. But every time you see a shift there's great potential for a slip. When you feel a shift coming on in your writing, remember: the slip you save may be your own.

Stamp out slips in our time: Avoid shifts in subject, number, tense, point of view, and sex.

Structure Your Writing

6

If you've ever taken the time to review your company's organization, you have probably noticed several things about its structure. First, you may have observed the complexity of the corporation. Even the structure of small U.S. corporations is remarkably intricate and specialized. Second, you may have noticed that the hierarchical order of the structure makes it easy for you to determine both the corporate power structure and personnel functions. And, third, you probably realized how far most of us have to go to make it to the top.

PARALLELISM

At the heart of any good corporate organizational chart is a simple, effective technique: parallelism. Department heads stand next to department heads, and production clerks are grouped with typists. In writing, the basic principle of parallelism is this: similar and logically related ideas must be expressed in the same grammatical structure. Parallelism is vital to any good piece of writing because it leads the reader directly from likeness in form to the likeness in both content and function. Consider how quickly you can tell "Who's Who" in your corporation just by position on the organizational chart.

Parallelism is effective because it:

- Forces the writer to think logically
- Gives structure to writing
- Makes sense to readers

Probably the most important effect of parallelism is to make the sentence easy to understand.

Unparallel Lines: The line supervisors' responsibilities are training of new salesmen, to develop new customers, and support upper-level management's decisions.

Parallel Lines: The line supervisors' responsibilities are to train new salesmen, to develop new customers, and to support upper-level management's decisions.

In the first example the grammatical forms of the three responsibilities are different and confusing: *training, to develop,* and (to) *support.* Note that all are verb forms that act as nouns, but because they look and sound different, readers cannot easily understand how to order or evaluate the responsibilities of the line supervisors. The second example keeps the responsibilities parallel and creates the immediate impression that each has equal weight and each is critical to the job: *to train, to develop,* and *to support.*

Here are some quick tips designed to keep your writing in line:

- Keep elements in a series parallel:
  Not: The manager is *young, has little experience,* and *not very patient.*

  But: The new manager is *young, inexperienced,* and *impatient.*

- Follow correlative conjunctions (not only/but also, either/or, (either/nor, etc.) with parallel forms:
  Not: The new corporate treasurer was known not only *for keen wit,* but also *as a financial wizard.*

  But: The new corporate treasurer was known not only *as a keen wit,* but also *as a financial wizard.*

- Use the parallel structure with coordinating conjunctions (and, but, yet, etc.):
  Not: She likes *to play tennis* and *running.*

  But: She likes *tennis* and *running.*

- Repeat, where appropriate, prepositions, verbs, or conjunctions to maintain parallel construction and to clarify meaning.
  Not: The new account manager was given tips *by* other company executives who liked her *and* the vice president who was her mother.

  But: The new account executive was given tips *by* other company executives, who liked her, *and by* the vice president, who was her mother.

Parallelism brings more than order to business writing. It brings elegance—creating rhythms and language patterns that have an almost musical appeal. Unparallel structures, by contrast, have all the appeal of cacophony.

Solid organization has a strong effect on the reader's opinion of both the writer and the writer's ideas. If an argument is logically presented, the reader is more likely to pronounce it sensible—and support it—even if it is not a particularly good argument. By contrast, if the plan is illogically presented and lacks a coherent structure, the reader will assume it is ill-conceived and unworkable, even if it is a superb plan.

THE BEGINNING, MIDDLE, AND END OF STRUCTURE

All writing must begin and end, regardless of its ordering in between. The reader, however, has certain expectations of order and completion that the writer must meet to be effective. In general, one basic format serves any approach well: where possible, have a beginning, a middle, and an end.

The Beginning

Your opening paragraph should draw readers directly into the writing. It should be interesting and inviting and it should set the rhythms and patterns of the piece that will follow. It should have a come-on that is provocative and promises some payoff—and it should also introduce your thesis or main idea. In sum, the opening paragraph sets up the basis and direction for the rest of the composition by inviting the reader to continue reading and by introducing the thesis. Consider this beginning of a short story about a new editor:

> The new editor walked through the newsroom today. After speaking to each of the desk editors and greeting some of the reporters, he went into his glass-partitioned office. He carefully took off his suit jacket and neatly hung it on the coat rack. After methodically rolling up his shirt sleeves, he sharpened five pencils to fine points and sat straight at his desk. The reporters, watching this out of the corner of their eyes, began to reread their stories carefully because the editor's reputation for ruthless editing had preceded him.

This opening paragraph introduces someone that neither the reporters nor the readers know. Being new automatically invites human inquiry. The reader wants to know more, especially if the editor is as tough as his reputation—which, by the way, is the story's thesis.

The Middle

The middle section should develop the thesis. You may choose your own direction, but in some way you must keep the reader interested and informed. Generally, the middle paragraphs can develop the thesis through opinions, both pro and con, specific details, statistics, or any relative information that will serve to inform, entertain, persuade, or motivate the reader. These paragraphs carry the bulk of the writing and they must be well done or they'll lose the reader's interest. Make sure these paragraphs are connected with good transition sentences so the reader isn't distracted along the way. See how the following middle paragraphs of the short story about the new editor develop the thesis through specific details:

> The first column to reach the new editor's desk was the social page. Traditionally the sacred cow of the paper, this column had enjoyed editorial immunity for years. But this editor was obviously no timid notary. Fear came into the hearts of the awaiting reporters as they watched him wear down two of his five pencils. When he finished, the editor called for a copy boy to pick up the column and return it.
>
> Everyone tensely watched the social reporter read the editorial comments. Soon he began to smile, then openly chuckle. He put down the blue-marked paper and went to the cafeteria for a cup of coffee.

These two paragraphs clearly support the thesis that this new editor is methodical: we have watched him wear down two of his sharpest pencils and promptly return the marked-up copy to the social reporter. And the new editor certainly seems to be living up to his reputation as a ruthless editor. But why is the reporter smiling at such ruthlessness? The reader must go on—curiosity, you know.

The End

The final paragraph should bring the thesis to some sort of resolution. Again you can be as creative as you wish here: just remember that the reader has invested time in your writing and is looking for some sort of payoff. Often a twist at the end is effective because it comes as a nice surprise and is much like a bonus dividend for the reader. Now let's see what happens to our story as we get the payoff:

> Gradually several of the more inquisitive reporters created a reason to drift over to the social reporter's desk. The page, they noticed, was covered with blue editing symbols, but the final comments at the

bottom of the page showed a new side of the editor: "Pete, I've always been a fan of yours. You get the scoop even before my wife does, and that's no small task. If I didn't edit this closely, however, you can bet we'd both get a call from her.

The final paragraph reinforces the thesis that our new editor is tough, but it also reveals a secret: he's got a good sense of humor—and anyone can live with that.

GENERAL TO SPECIFIC

When you want to hit the reader between the eyes, present your conclusion first. By doing so, you develop a "show-me" attitude among your readers which focuses attention on your central idea or thesis. In effect, an initial challenge is thrown down between the readers and the writer. If you can substantiate the conclusion with facts that convince the reader, you'll be successful.

As an example, if you were trying to convince a customer to buy your computer, you might start by writing that it's one of the top five industrial computers on the market. Of course the reader says, "Top five, huh? Who says so besides you?" If you can show the reader *who* says so, you'll have a powerful sales document. If not, you'd better revise your approach fast.

Leading with the conclusion only holds the reader for a short span of time. You have to be able to back it up with quick and convincing facts—or your lead will be overtaken by disbelief and boredom.

SPECIFIC TO GENERAL

Have you ever had to break an appointment? Say "no" to someone? Refute an argument? If you have, chances are you used the specific-to-general approach. This technique generates a persuasive argument and is most effective when you anticipate a skeptical or negative reaction. By gradually building up to the conclusion with fact upon fact, you inadvertently program readers to accept your conclusion. This technique is more subtle and less emotional than a direct statement and should be employed for occasions that require letters of refusal and letters of regret.

THE CHRONOLOGICAL METHOD

The chronological method is popular because humans live in time, remember things as they happened in time, and like to order events in time. This method usually begins with the earliest significant date of an event and works forward to the most recent date. Date sequence, or chronology, provides straight history to the reader and is a good method to use for a background or an overview piece of writing. It is also effectively employed in creating historical files, documenting personnel folders, or writing progress letters. The chronological method conveys a sense of history and is best used to document the sequence of events.

Chronology is generally easy to follow, but remember to keep the journey short: if you don't limit your time frame, you'll lose your reader somewhere in the past. When you're going to talk about the state of modern relationships between men and women, don't start with Adam and Eve if you expect readers to be awake by the time you get to the 20th century.

THE REVERSE CHRONOLOGICAL METHOD

This method starts from the most recent event and moves backwards in time. It is best used to jog the reader's memory. You might use it in memoranda when you're trying to remind the boss about something in the past.

CAVEAT ON STRUCTURE

Remember, structure does not command—it acts as a guide. You can outline a structure then fill in the details. Or, you can write off the top of your head, then extract your structure. Many writers don't know what they mean until they see what they say. Above all, don't lock yourself into just one formula or you'll be as bored by writing as your writing is boring. Certainly, structuring devices like *underlining, capitalization, headings, numbered paragraphs, indentation,* and *columns,* as well as structured approaches like general to specific, specific to general, chronological, and reverse chronological, will help bring order and clarity to writing. Don't, however, let order or structure become your master. The best advice might be the adage, "all things in moderation."

Write with Style 7

Most inexperienced writers think that great authors receive divine language from some greater force in the universe. Great authors, they think, sit entranced at desks as well-polished sentences flow from their quills. The fact is writing's a *skill,* learned and refined through a process of hard work. If, then, an experienced writer works easily because of constant practice, inexperienced writers should react to their own difficulties by practicing—not by mumbling about God-given gifts.

THE PROCESS OF WRITING

Writing is not a onetime or sudden event. It is a process—a series of steps necessary to achieve a finished piece of effective writing. Collectively, these steps make up the process of writing:

- Selecting

First, you must select an idea that will interest you. This idea should readily link with your previous experiences, ideas, and interests, and it should strike a nerve deep within you. In other words, you must select an idea that has enough meaning to you that it will stimulate your interest for a sustained period of time. This initial process of selecting the right idea is developed through practice. Like playing a sport or mastering a skill, the more you do it, the better you become.

- Exploring

Once you've selected the idea, give it to your unconscious mind for a day or two—if you have the luxury of a little time. Stranger than fiction, this activity is an effective one: by choosing an idea firmly, then ignoring it, it will rattle around freely in the mind and link up with connected but forgotten things in your brain's deep storage. Soon these "things" will begin to surface in the conscious mind. At the most unexpected moments you'll be struck by relationships between new ideas and old experiences—and you should record these relationships as they occur to you, as notes, in outline form, even as long, windy paragraphs. Sometimes these ideas will work and sometimes not, but they will always give you a good place to start. This step is an initial exploration of that marvelous computer called your brain. A scan search of your unconscious mind is essential if you're to take advantage of your life experiences in your writing.

• Scrawling

This part is fun. Sit down with a piece of paper in the typewriter or under your pencil and type or write anything that comes into your head. Don't stop for neat typing or penmanship. Don't stop to correct spelling, to punctuate, or to complete sentences—just get your ideas on paper. I call this step "scrawling" because it's somewhere *beneath* writing, and it describes the kind of freeflowing activity that I hope you'll have the courage to try. Once you've gotten the hang of it, you'll enjoy it—and you'll discover you have more and better ideas than you ever would have thought. If you're used to editing your writing line by line, you may at first find it hard to scrawl. Letting a misspelled word or an incomplete sentence stand until the whole idea is out is almost impossible at first for some people. You will, however, benefit from this technique if only because it gives concrete forms to vague ideas. If you had to fix a faulty widget, would you rather have the widget in your hands or hear a description of it?

• Surveying

Now, survey what you've written and begin to look for informational holes—places in your scrawling that seem to lack depth or substance. Edit the scrawling first on a grand scale: just label similar groups of ideas with the same letter or number to help you establish how much information you have in a certain area. This technique will show you graphically and quickly where you need work. If you only have a few letters or numbers in an important area, you'll need more research there.

• Hunting

Hunt out books, magazines, papers, and letters. Go to friends, aunts, uncles, and cousins to find the information you need to fill the holes in your writing. At this point you may realize that your idea is too big or too little for your particular purpose. You may find that you'll have to limit your topic or choose a new one. If you take the time to hunt properly, you'll define your limits now and prevent a lot of wasted time and writing later.

- Writing

Once you've gathered all your documentation, start writing. Write as fast as you can to get the ideas on paper; because you are armed with facts this time, your writing will be more substantive. The result will be your first draft, so leave wide margins all around and double—even triple—space it. When you finish the draft, let it sit for a day if you have the time.

- Editing

Edit your initial draft to get a more concise, accurate, and readable expression of your ideas. Scribble notes up and down the page; cross out phrases and entire sentences; draw arrows over, around, and through words. Then put your writing aside for awhile to get a little distance from it. You need the distance to clear your mind—and to prepare you to make more changes.

- Rewriting

Rewriting is as arduous as it is productive. As a rule, the quality of writing improves in proportion to the number of times a piece is rewritten. Nevertheless, the editing and rewriting processes are painful because they force you to give up writing that you like, but which doesn't fit. Saying goodbye to well-crafted phrases or witty ideas isn't easy. Remember, too, the longer you work with a piece of writing, the harder it is to give any of it up.

- Testing

Now it's time to test your writing with people whose opinion you respect. And the more people the better. Be careful not to prepare the members of your test group before they read the piece, but tell them to be honest and heartless. Then when your writing is returned, you'll have to decide on what stays, goes, or needs to be rewritten. This step in the process of writing is often neglected by new writers but seldom by experienced writers. Repeat this step after different drafts and as often as possible before the deadline.

- Ending

At some point you have to finish the writing—if only to meet a deadline. If there were not deadlines, many writers would rewrite indefinitely and probably go mad in the process. Rewriting is only limited by your patience; as a rule of thumb, however, when your writing begins to come back with few or no editing remarks from other readers, it's probably ready for the final draft, proofreading, and publication. Don't be surprised if you have mixed feelings when you submit it.

TIPS FOR SUCCESSFUL WRITING

Now that you are aware of the entire writing process *in general,* consider some practical tips for writing that gets the job done at work:

Know What You Want

Take a moment before you begin and reduce your writing purpose to a simple sentence: "I want this customer to know that our company is sorry for our mistake," or "I want our manufacturer to know that we are angry he missed our deadline because it cost us money." By doing this, you will clarify your purpose and stick to the mission at hand. This purpose sentence serves as a guide for your rough outline and gives direction to your communication.

Remember That the Reader Doesn't Have Much Time

Business people are pushed for time. They have many and constant demands placed on them. Don't contribute to their stress by drafting a communication that requires a $100 investment for a 10-cent problem. Keep your writing clear, direct, well-organized, and short. If not, chances are it might just end up at the bottom of the pile or, worse yet, in the trash can, unread.

Lead with the Main Point

Lead with your strong point. Don't make the reader go on a treasure hunt to find your gem. Don't bury the main point in the middle of a paragraph or the reader might miss it. To discover what your main point or main sentence is, read a paragraph. Now decide which sentence would be the last one you would toss out. That sentence is your main point for the paragraph.

Make Writing Easy to Read

Make your writing pleasant to read by using some simple techniques:

- Indent main points in a paragraph
- Underline for extra stress
- Use lists and bullets
- Don't fill the page with typing—use white space to rest the reader's eyes; for example, skip lines between paragraphs
- Use subheadings to break space and ensure clarity

Think of things you've read that appeal to you. Save those examples and study them, and use the devices you like in them.

Keep the Reader's Needs in Mind

If you want your writing to be understood, keep the reader's needs, demands, concerns, and point of view in mind as you write. Avoid unfamiliar language or terms, and address questions you know the reader will logically have about your subject. In short, follow the golden rule of writing: help the reader in ways that you would want to be helped. Remember, the reason you are writing is to communicate something to the reader.

Speak Directly to the Reader

To avoid stilted and formal language that can put the reader off, pretend that you are speaking directly to the reader. A dictaphone or tape recorder may be useful. Be careful, however. Don't forget to edit your conversation strictly, since speech can be too informal, too chatty, and too sloppy.

Don't Overwrite

Consider the impact of the Declaration of Independence, the Preamble of the Constitution, the Lord's Prayer, and the Gettysburg Address. All of these written pieces are short but powerful. Don't be afraid to cut.

Keep It Simple

Never use two words when one will do. Never use a paragraph when a sentence will do. Always strive for brevity and simplicity.

Don't Write Alone

Always get someone else to criticize your writing objectively before you submit it. The more you work with your writing the less objective you become, so ask someone else to read specifically for clarity and accuracy. The only thing better than one person editing is two people editing. We don't live in a vacuum, so why write in one?

Avoid Injecting Your Opinion

Stick to facts in business writing. Rarely does the reader want your gratuitous opinion on a particular matter. Deal with facts and avoid the unmistakable mark of egotism in your writing.

Avoid Qualifiers and Vague Modifiers

Don't use modifiers that almost say what you want when you can find ones that are exact.

Close	*Exact*
The shirt was very expensive.	The shirt cost $300.
The train was very late.	The train was 4 hours late.

Don't Use Cliches

Worn-out expressions can wear a reader's patience thin. Avoid hackneyed phrases and use direct, fresh language:

Trite	*Natural*
First and foremost	First
All around the mulberry bush	Everywhere

Avoid Exaggeration

Avoid the superlative when you write. The greatest, the worst, the prettiest all leave you open to exception. To avoid arguments from the reader, avoid overstating your position.

Sum It Up

The last paragraph should summarize what you've been discussing. It should tell the reader what you want done or what you will do.

Don't forget the Tips for Successful Writing:

- Know what you want
- Remember that the reader doesn't have much time
- Lead with your main point
- Make writing easy to read
- Keep the reader's needs in mind
- Speak directly to the reader
- Don't overwrite
- Keep writing simple
- Don't write alone
- Avoid injecting your opinion
- Avoid qualifiers or vague modifiers
- Don't use cliches or trite expressions
- Avoid exaggeration
- Sum it up

Manage Your Writing Through
Dictation and Editing

8

With the advent of telecommunications and computers, the pace of business has quickened and businesses have become more efficient. Because of the faster pace, business writing has trouble staying timely and effective. To keep up with the information flood and the speed of computers in the '80s, managers must learn two basic word-management survival tools: dictation and effective editing. Managers must be able not only to express themselves in writing quickly and efficiently, but also to edit the work of others with the same effectiveness.

DICTATION—A MUST IN BUSINESS

Dictation equipment has become as commonplace as coffee cups in today's offices. Go into any executive's office and you'll probably find a dictation machine perched confidently on the desk or credenza. In fact, the office word-processing system is usually based on tape recordings of dictated material. Necessarily, then, dictation is the first skill new employees must learn to do their jobs.

For those of you who are used to paper-and-pencil rough drafts— and you are the majority—the initial exposure to dictation is frightening. First-timers in particular are left in a near-catatonic state, clenching the microphone and stammering to get out the first word. After practice and constant use, however, words begin to trickle, then flow, and then, unfortunately, flood.

The principal advantage and disadvantage of dictation are the same: it's as easy as conversation. On the plus side, dictation offers a natural way to get ideas down on paper since most of us are already skilled at talking. On the other hand, like conversation, dictation tends to ramble and produces far more words than necessary. The trick is to maximize the advantages and minimize the disadvantages.

Advantages of Dictation

- Dictation Is Quick

Probably three to five times faster than writing, dictation gives you a draft-well before you could rough out an introduction in pencil.

- Dictation Is Timely

Because of its speed and because it is available, you can dictate notes immediately after a meeting while your memory is fresh.

- Dictation Is Efficient

You don't waste time transmitting your ideas through a mechanical medium—scrawling out words on paper or plunking out letters on a typewriter. Instead, you simply speak, projecting ideas and information as you think of them.

- Dictation Is Cost Effective

Because it eliminates the need for a live stenographer and takes so little executive time, dictation equipment provides today's companies with the cheapest basis for a word-processing system.

- Dictation Gives an Immediate Sense of Accomplishment

The fast process immediately gratifies the person dictating. One moment you have an idea, and the next moment it's on paper.

- Dictation Relieves Stress

Dictation takes the "monkey" off your back because it's so effortless and fast. By being able to get an idea on paper so quickly, you never have time to generate the tension associated with waiting to commit an idea to paper.

- Dictation Systems Are Highly Developed

Dictation systems have been in operation for years. Now they are efficient and sophisticated enough to meet the needs of any writer willing to give them a chance.

Disadvantages of Dictation

- Dictation Can Become A Substitute for Preparation

Executives often dictate before their ideas are formed—using the process, in fact, to decide what they want to say. Their dictation consequently is ninety percent wasted words.

- Verbal Pauses Clutter Dictation

When we speak, we all use pause words to give ourselves time to think about what we want to say next: these are the *ers,* the *you-knows,* the *ums,* the *let's sees,* and typists can easily delete these obvious pauses, but they would hesitate to cut out pause clusters like: *at this point in time, as I was saying,* etc. Letters and reports, as a result, are filled with such clutter.

- Dictation Can Cause "Literary Laziness"

The burden of transcribing falls on the shoulders of the typist. Because typists check words for spelling and will even help with the editing, many dictators get sloppy and develop "literary laziness," refusing to check word usage and grammar themselves during the dictation process.

- Dictation Is Often Not Rewritten

Here is the single greatest disadvantage of dictation. Though many of today's executives dictate, few take time to rewrite the original draft. Without undergoing the essential steps of editing and rewriting, dictated material can't help but reflect the imprecision of speech. Dictation is the best place to start drafting, but the worst place to end the writing process.

Now that you know the advantages and disadvantages of dictation, take a look at the net results:

Bottom Line for Good Dictation
- Start with a Rough Outline to Give Yourself and Your Dictation Direction
- Treat Initial Dictation Only as a Rough Draft, Not as a Final Draft
- Edit Dictation Ruthlessly—Then Edit It Again
- Remember That Dictation Is Only Part of the Writing Process

Dictation is a quick, efficient, and useful tool for the business writer. Used correctly, it is an invaluable asset to the company.

THE EDITING PROCESS

Editing the Writing of Others

Editing and reviewing the writing of other writers requires skill and diplomacy. Editing can be a traumatic experience for both writer and editor. Though writers may tell you they don't mind your changes, you can be assured that they do—at least a little. Because writing expresses an individual personality, writers take personal offense at suggested changes. Editors, on the other hand, see their well-intended remarks formed against them, and wonder why they bothered to help. Before listing some techniques of editing, let's look at several general caveats about the process.

- Be a Gentle Editor

Use unemotional words unless you're praising the work. Don't use words like "awful" or "terrible." Treat writing as if it is the child of the writer. Use phrases like "please clarify" or "expand this idea." If you take out the emotion, tension will stay low and productivity high.

- Be a Positive Editor

Try to begin your overall editorial comments by pointing out what works well in that particular piece of writing. Then show how and where it can be strengthened to make it even better.

- Work Collaboratively with the Writer

Working together, the editor and writer form a powerful and effective team. Keep the editing process collaborative and enjoy the fruits of mutual success.

- Use a Stylebook for Consistency

A number of excellent writing stylebooks are available on the market. Use the stylebook of Chicago University, of the Washington Post, of the New York Times, or of some other agency, but do use one standard book—and use it throughout the office. Be sure everyone has a copy, and insist everyone complies with it. Conformance to a standard stylebook will give your business a distinctive and effective writing voice.

Editing Tips: Clarity, Conformity, Tone, Logic, Accuracy

When you edit someone else's writing, remember these simple but effective techniques:

- Edit for Clarity, Not Style

All writers have their own particular style. Limit style only when clarity is at stake.

- Edit for Conformity to Company Standards

As a reviewing official, you must understand and enforce company practices, standards, and policies. Closely review the writing of newer, less experienced employees.

- Edit for an Even Tone

Take out emotion-charged words. Keep the tone of all business communication forthright, reasoned, and professional. Emotional writing invites overreaction and causes problems.

- Edit for Logic and Organization

Readers, being human, understand and expect logic. The structure of a piece of writing must, therefore, organize and sustain the ideas in it. Edit structure to ensure that the writing in it will be understood by the greatest possible number of people.

- Edit for the Reader

Readers should be treated not only as clients but also as friends. Apply the golden rule of writing: Write for others as you would have them write for you.

- Edit for Fact

Challenge questionable matters of fact—because you can be sure readers will. Both writer and editor must guarantee the accuracy of facts.

Editing and Proofreading Symbols

The following proofreading symbols were devised as short-form directions to the printers. They are standard in the United States and will make your job of editing infinitely easier:

Symbols	*Results*
Delete this error	Delete this error
Place a comma here please	Place a comma here, please
Use a colon for the following	Use a colon for the following:
Always capitalize the capitol	Always capitalize the Capitol
Use figures for numbers like twenty	Use figures for numbers like 20
Insert an apostrophe when its needed	Insert an apostrophe when it's needed
Indent new paragraphs	Indent new paragraphs
Insert mising letters	Insert missing letters

Editing marks	Corrected text
Link words like news⁀paper	Link words like newspaper
Join letters to make sen⁀se	Join letters to make sense
Transpose words these for clarity	Transpose these words for clarity
Link this copy and what follows	Link this copy and what follows
Transpose these lettesrn	Transpose these letters
Insert words *necessary*	Insert necessary words
Use boldface capitals for the first chapter:	Use boldface capitals for the first chapter:
the beginning BFC	**THE BEGINNING**
Use lowercase letter Here *lc*	Use lowercase letter here
Insert a period⊗	Insert a period.
Spell the name Joans as written *CQ*	Spell the name Joans as written
Spell out the numbers ①thru ⑩	Spell out the numbers one thru ten

The relationship between the writer and the manager/editor is often determined by the style of editing. Editing can be an intrusive technique that affects adversely the attitude and productivity of the writer, or it can be an effective technique if the manager/editor is gentle, positive, and supportive. When editing, the manager/editor should edit for: conformity to company policies, consistency of tone, organization of structure, and, finally, foundation of fact.

Good writing is a collaborative effort of both writer and editor. When the two combine harmoniously, writing improves measurably. Effective editing is a must for any manager in the '80s who wants to project the company's message well.

Write to Your Audience 9

All writing is communication, and communication means two or more people involved in an exchange of ideas. Writing is not solely the province of the writer: it is jointly owned by the writer and the reader. Writing itself is thus only a part of the process of communication. Not until the reader has absorbed the writing is that process complete.

Readers, as an integral part of the process, must be addressed with deliberation. Yet the reading audience, unfortunately, is often forgotten by writers. This chapter will profile the audience of written business communications and define the kind of relationship that should exist between the writer and the audience.

PUT PEOPLE IN YOUR WRITING

People do things. People take action, respond, comply with regulations. And companies are nothing more than gatherings of people. Unfortunately, when companies write to other companies, they use sterile language, language that dehumanizes the communication that makes it cold, lifeless, and boring. It's incredible when you think about it. We're trying to inform, explain, or motivate, yet we linguistically approach the situation as if it were a rare disease requiring a surgically sterile isolation. We put on masks, sterile gloves, and gowns to hide ourselves, and even drape the patient so that both patient and surgeon have completely lost their identities—then we attempt to enter into the most personal thing we do as humans: communication.

When we speak, we unthinkingly use a personal touch. First, we address the person and not the company. Second, we get to know people a little before we make demands of them. Third, we assimilate knowledge about them that helps us shape our communications system to meet their needs. We look at how they dress, and we listen to what they say and how they say it (dialect, intonation, diction). In fact, we absorb a remarkable amount of information about an individual before we ever speak a word. The entire process might take only a fraction of a second, but it happens nonetheless, and it's crucial to good communication. In general, the more time you have to assess your audience, the better the chance that you'll get your point across.

In writing, however, we ignore the reader or audience and focus on the theme—but what *we* want is not necessarily what the reader wants or needs. It's here where writing fails. Consider how easily the problem can be corrected:

- Address Your Communication to a Person

Avoid addressing a letter to "Dear Sir," or "Gentlemen," or "Dear Madam." These people are all dead—in fact, they never lived. They're ciphers, nonentities—and they dehumanize the person who receives the letter. Take the time to find out a name and send your letter to a real person: "Dear Mr. Johnson," "Dear Harry," "Dear Somebody."

- Be a Somebody Yourself

Let the reader know you're a real person with a name, a sense of humor, and ideas. Relate to your reader in human terms just as you would at a social gathering. Your language should reflect your personality. Tell stories, relate interesting situations—especially humorous ones—to illustrate a point. Don't shy away from using "I" or "me" or "we"—only "the company" is an "it."

- Assess What the Audience Needs

Most people will accept or do something that has a payback for them. Motivation begins at home. If you've done your homework before you write, you should have some idea about what motivates your readers—and what doesn't. Armed with such intelligence you can write to their needs and be fairly sure of a good reception.

- Know Exactly What You Want

Decide in a nutshell what you want your communication to accomplish and what action, if any, you want the reader to take. If you're not sure what you want, you'll never galvanize your reader.

- Use Appropriate Language

Just as you would never send a letter written in English to a reader who does not speak the language, so too you should never send a message to an audience that won't completely understand it. Avoid flowery and pretentious language. Use language that the reader uses. You can find out the appropriate style by reading and studying some of his or her correspondence. Become a bit of a detective and see how much you can learn from the type of language the reader has used. If you have no writing samples, make notes the next time you speak with the reader. You'll hear idioms, rhythms, and regional expressive style after which you can pattern your own writing. If the reader identifies with you—even stylistically—he'll give your proposals greater consideration.

To sum up, these initial steps will help put people in your writing:

- Write to a person, not a company
- Identify yourself as a person, not a company
- Assess and meet the reader's needs
- Know what you want
- Use appropriate language

AUDIENCE TYPES

How many audiences are there? As many as there are people and groups of people. In business, however, correspondents fall into two general types: Internal and External. Internal audiences are those people to whom you must write inside the company: subordinates, superiors, and peers. External audiences are those people you write outside the company: consumers, customers, vendors, competitors, the news media, the government.

WRITING WITHIN THE ORGANIZATION

Let's begin inside the company before we venture outside:

Writing to Superiors

Communicating with the boss is essential to your survival in the company. Many of us must communicate daily with the boss on a number of pressing subjects. How well we communicate our ideas and thoughts to him or her—whether in written or spoken form—largely determines our success or failure in the organization.

When writing to your boss, keep in mind the general tips on writing: what does he or she like? Is he or she formal or informal? Can he or she accept slang? Does he or she have a sense of humor, and if so, what type? The better you know your boss, the better you can tailor your language to suit his or her style.

- Tips for Writing to the Boss:
—Ask a third party who knows the boss to read your memo and give you an impartial but informed read-out of the boss's reaction.
—Enlist the aid of the boss' secretary where possible. He or she can give you valuable insight into the boss, his or her moods, needs, and wants.
—Read the boss' most recent memos to get a sense of diction, style, and tone from them.
—Look on the boss' bookshelves and at pictures or sayings hanging on the wall of the office. These can give you good personality clues, ones you need if the boss is new and you don't know him or her well.

Writing to Peers

Communicating laterally in an organization is perhaps the most difficult task of all because we've been trained from earliest days to compete—not communicate—with our peers. Business is a competitive arena, and after all those years on the athletic field, we are trained to beat out the other person, to seek the advantage, and always to keep score.

If you don't moderate a one-upsmanship approach with your peers, however, you'll find yourself on the losing side.

- Tips for Writing to Peers:
—Keep language direct and forthright.
—Establish what you want and how getting it will benefit your peers. Your peers will react negatively to a "sales job." Hit them straight with what you want to avoid arousing their competitive instincts.
—Attempt to work collaboratively with peers. If you can persuade potential competitors to join you in a project, it will be doubly successful, for you'll have their support instead of their resistance.
—Finally, offer alternatives in case your first idea is rejected.

Writing to Subordinates

The bottom line of all work is getting the job done. Nevertheless, the way managers motivate subordinates to do the job determines which one is successful and which mediocre. Managers write to subordinates for two reasons: first, because when the idea is in the manager's mind the subordinate is not around to discuss it; second, to document instructions. Because most forms of performance rating are based on written documentation, managers must put instructions and incidental evaluations on paper.

When writing notes or instructions to those below you on the corporate structure, a few hints will prove helpful in getting the job done while retaining good rapport.

- Tips for Writing to Subordinates:

—Write collectively. Include the subordinates on your team. Use words like *we, us,* and *our.*

—Instill a sense of corporate ownership. Convince subordinates that their role is integral to the overall performance of the company.

—Be polite, not patronizing. Simple words of courtesy help get the work done. Thank subordinates for their work; ask for their help; and seek out their ideas.

—Write out praise. If subordinates have done a good job for you, let them know it in writing. Be specific with your praise so that you don't sound like an insincere backslapper.

—Tell them when you're not pleased. The sword cuts both ways, but when you criticize, be specific and attack only specific acts, not general personality traits. Specifics help the employee focus on and correct his error and keep him from taking the criticism personally.

—Use humor when possible. The business world is far too impersonal. Humor, however, conveys a humanness that everyone, especially subordinates, can appreciate. Punctuate your writing with humor; save the somber stuff for those times that demand it.

—Be creative in everyday writing. Short memos and notes to employees can be creative. Don't miss the opportunity to exercise your mind and your pen. Try to find different ways of saying things. Try a new style or use a new word just to practice it.

Writing to subordinates can be a valuable exercise and opportunity in the writing process as well as an indispensable managerial tool. Too often we avoid writing and miss that opportunity. Writing is a skill that must be practiced or it is lost. Seizing the chance wherever we can ensures us that we'll at least get some practice. Remember, when writing to subordinates, don't make it a boring task, make it creative.

WRITING TO THE PUBLIC

As we climb the corporate ladder, we write increasingly to people outside the company. It's a fact of business life that the higher we climb, the more we affect the world around us and the more we need to correspond with that world.

There are numerous external audiences with whom we might have to correspond. The following are just a few of those:

- The Public

Customers are surely one of the most important groups that we address. Without them, business doesn't happen. When responding to consumers, be direct, forthright, and accurate, and ensure that answers to specific problems are correct and courteous. Be sure not to use patronizing language or you might lose your most valuable asset—a cash-paying customer. Be sure to avoid impersonal answers—remember that the consumer is a person just like you.

- Vendors

It takes many people to keep a business healthy, and vendors are vital to corporate longevity. Those who supply the daily goods that are necessary to our job are vital to us and should be treated personally. When writing to them, keep in mind that even though they're paid for their services, like employees they also need to be told when they do well and when they don't perform. Writing provides the occasion and means to express pleasure or displeasure. Your diction may vary, of course, depending upon your relationship with the vendor. Certainly your diction may vary from dealing with a new vendor to one with whom you've been associated for years.

- The News Media

The Fourth Estate can make or break a company. Handling the media has become a well-defined art and a method to corporate survival in today's information-hungry society. How your company responds during a strike or disaster may be the public's only view of your operation besides buying your products. The image you reflect may make your public like or dislike you, which can mean a swing in profits. Make sure that your dealings with the press come only after a great deal of preparation. Write out in detail your considered responses to anticipated questions. Have someone inside the company play the devil's advocate and rehearse your responses. Spontaneity is not usually a good substitute for preparation. Make sure that your responses are honestly what you believe, and then rehearse your delivery. Remember that your delivery in this case is as important as your written preparation. When the writers take notes or when the cameras and tape recorders whir, make sure you're prepared.

The number of external audiences are almost infinite. All of them have some bearing on the company life and, therefore, must be effectively communicated with. When writing to any audience, whether as big as the government or as small as a one-man business, remember some of the general tips discussed earlier:

- Write to a person, not a company
- Be a person yourself
- Know what the reader needs
- Know what you want
- Use appropriate language

Writers compete for a reader's valuable time. To be a winner and an effective communicator, a writer must strike a bond with the reader. To create this bond, it's the writer's job to do a background investigation on the audience well before putting pen to paper.

NOTES

NOTES

NOTES

NOTES